Disney
MICKEY
& FRIENDS

MEGA
Colouring

PaRragon

Bath · New York · Cologne · Melbourne · Delhi
Hong Kong · Shenzhen · Singapore · Amsterdam

The sea turtle taxi service is always free!

Even with flippers and tentacles you can still dance underwater.

This kite might get a little higher off the ground if Pluto would let go of the tail!

Daisy and Minnie share some tea and some laughs!

Working on a farm is hard work!

Donald's nephews go on a hay ride.

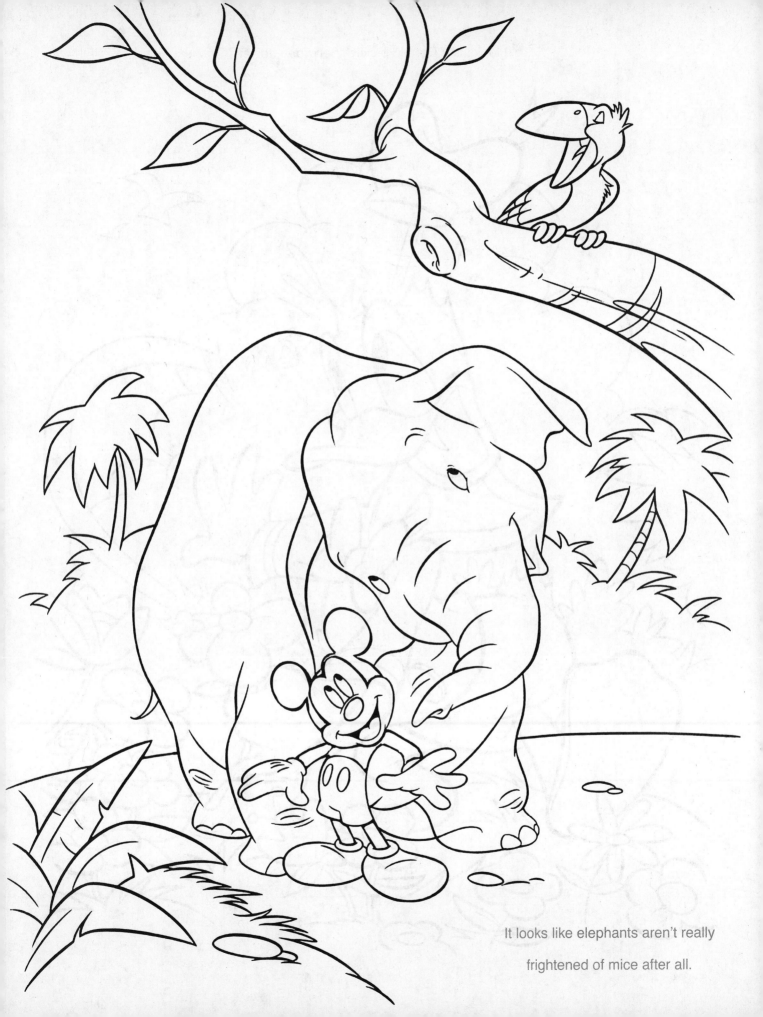

It looks like elephants aren't really

frightened of mice after all.

It looks like Donald picked the wrong flower!

All the ducks swim over as fast as they can when they see Goofy and his bucket.

With Donald around, crossing the street will always be safe.

Dolphins are extremely playful.

Minnie and an owl have a hooting contest.

Forest Ranger Donald doesn't like to see smoke in the trees.

Donald is ready to put out any fires!

Daisy asks Donald to push her even higher!

There's nothing Pluto likes more than playing in the park!

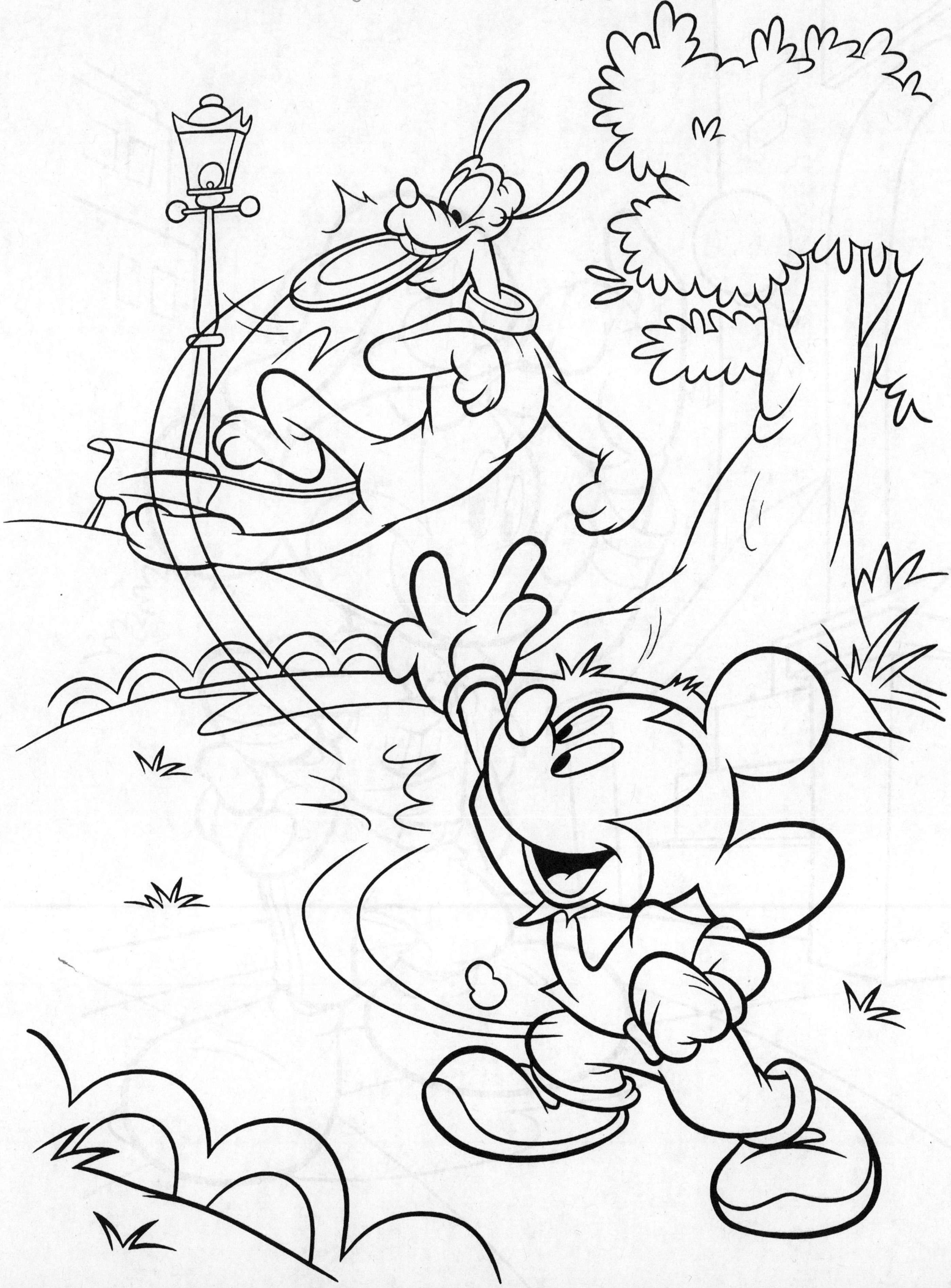

Mickey is here to protect and serve.

Cleaning up at the zoo just never seems to end!

Minnie loves to see her flowers grow.

Donald wanted to get a close-up of a doe.

The octopus doesn't look like it wants to share any of its treasure.

Children watch as Goody feeds the fish.

Don't you think Mickey makes a great cowboy?

Making cookies is easier when you have a good partner.

Donald and the parrot see eye to eye.

Donald needs a little more work on his act!

Daisy is quite the daredevil!

After a day out in the cold, Donald enjoys a hot drink in front of a roaring fire.

Making angels in the snow is always a good time.

Ice can be hard to walk on even when it's not flipping up in the air!

Donald makes a big splash with the whale.

It looks like Goofy is getting ready to throw the biggest snowball ever!

Pluto was hoping to build a snowdog, but he's still happy to help Mickey out with the snowman.

Donald gives a guided museum tour.

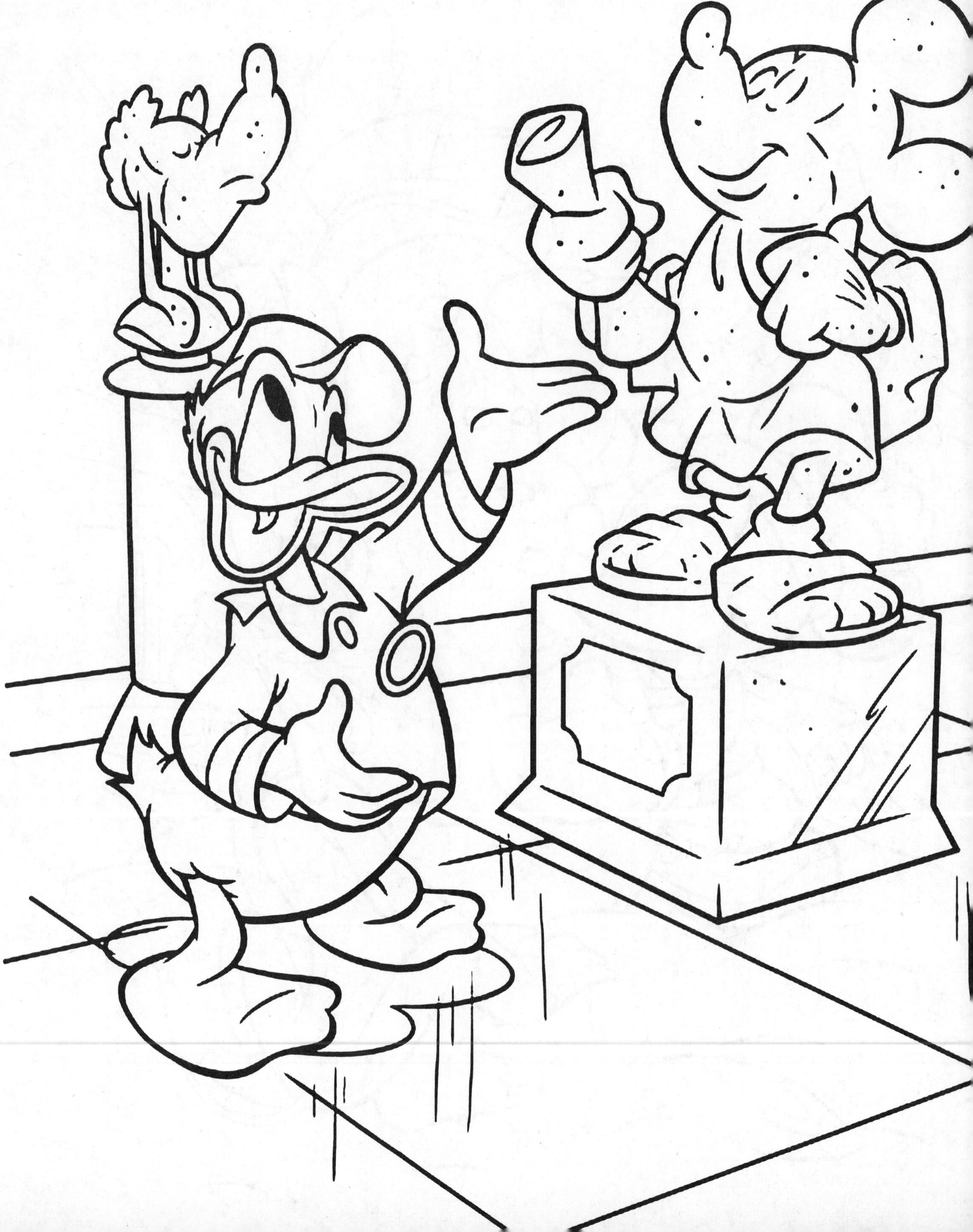

Scrooge McDuck really enjoys counting all his money.

Mickey is ready for takeoff!

When Donald asked the elephant for a drink this isn't what he had in mind!

Daisy would be happy to trade her ribbon for a butterfly anytime.

Goofy has to hustle to catch the train before it leaves the station.

Goofy is an excellent driver.

Daisy picked the wrong kind of hat for her walk through the jungle.

Mickey heads the ball past Donald!

It's a perfect day to take out a bicycle built for two.

Daisy finds an amazing pearl. Now if she

could only figure out how to wear it…

The flamingo gives Daisy a balancing lesson.

It's a good thing for Donald that there was one cone left.

Minnie is very happy with her purchases.

The best part about raking leaves is jumping in the pile when you're done!

Goofy lines up his shot before teeing off.

Goofy becomes a much better patient when a tasty treat is involved!

Minnie and Mickey settle into a swing after a busy day.

Goody takes a school photo.

There's nothing better on a hot day than a big ice cream cone.

Goofy seems to be missing something…

Pluto and a goat square off.

Goofy spins the pizza crust until it is ready to go in the oven.

Some dogs are really good swimmers.

Pluto thinks he has discovered a small cave.

Donald leads the Three Duck Band!

Daisy and Minnie kayak down a river together.

Goofy still needs a little work on his form.